This story is based on the life of Asma Rashed, a young mother of four who lives in the Zaatari refugee camp in Jordan.

Asma, like many other Syrian refugees, has lived through the struggles of war and displacement. Her resilience and determination led her to become a community leader who fights for better opportunities for her community and children.

Attending a We Love Reading training in the Zaatari camp in 2014 was a turning point for Asma. After receiving training on how to read aloud, she took it upon herself to share her skills, books and persevering spirit and desire for change with those around her.

# My Mama's Magic

Written By
Amina Awad

**Austin Macauley Publishers™**
LONDON · CAMBRIDGE · NEW YORK · SHARJAH

Copyright © Amina Awad 2022
Illustrated by Eshraq Othman

The rights of **Amina Awad** to be identified as author of this work and **Eshraq Othman** as the illustrator of this work, has been asserted by them in accordance with Federal Law No. (7) of UAE, Year 2002, Concerning Copyrights and Neighboring Rights.

All rights reserved. No part of this publication may be reproduced, stored in a retrieval system, or transmitted in any form or by any means, electronic, mechanical, photocopying, recording, or otherwise, without the prior permission of the publishers.

Any person who commits any unauthorized act in relation to this publication may be liable to legal prosecution and civil claims for damages.

The age category suitable for the books' contents has been classified and defined in accordance to the Age Classification System issued by the Ministry of Culture and Youth.

ISBN – 9789948806257 - (Paperback)

Application Number: MC-10-01-2872085
Age Classification: 10-12

First Published 2022
AUSTIN MACAULEY PUBLISHERS FZE
Sharjah Publishing City
P.O Box [519201]
Sharjah, UAE
www.austinmacauley.ae
+971 655 95 202

My mama has a secret.
She is a magician.
She uses magic to transform in the blink of an eye.
With a flicker of light, she can become anything!
She can become a genie in a lamp,
granting wishes to her visitors.
She can sprout wings with a tilt of her head
and sing the sweetest melody.
She can become a golden fish with shiny scales.
Or a butterfly breaking out of its cocoon.

I know you may not believe me.
But if you look closely and quietly,
you will see her magic at work.
When she cleans our tent, she can grow ten times her size.
She is a giant with a broom as her wand.
When the weather is stormy and wet,
her skin turns into scales.
She darts through the water, and can swim against
even the strongest tide.

My mother knows that magic is for everyone.
She gathers us all and lets us in on her secret.
In her grandest voice, she announces that she is revealing the source of her magic.
That's when she opens up a book.
And with a gasp, we see the magic gold dust spill out.
As she begins to read, she transforms from one page to the next.

Every week, we gather by the reading rocks to receive our weekly dose of magic.
We tumble over each other to get the best seat on the highest rock.
We wonder what magical adventure awaits us.
Will we see our old friends?
Or will we meet strange new creatures that will become our friends?

My mama's name is Asma.
But everyone in the camp knows her as the Hakawati,
the magic storyteller.
Whispers of her magic travel through camp.
Young and old eyes look at her with awe.
I can't wait until I am a Hakawati just like her.

You see, my mama wasn't always a Hakawati.
Not too long ago, she didn't have any magic.
She didn't know how to transform herself and the world around her.
She didn't know much about magic at all!

All that changed when one day a magician visited us.
She had a funny hat and a kind smile.
She gave my mom a secret package that was full of magic.
When my mom opened the package. . .
She found lots and lots of books!
Magic was floating off the books in clouds of golden dust.
The older magician told Mama that the best way to use the magic of storytelling was to share it with others.
And so my mother did just that.

My mama read…and read…and read.
Until she mastered the magic of storytelling.
Then she began to share it.
Everyone began to feel the presence of magic throughout the camp.
And it made my mama very happy.

My mama's magic takes us to cities we have never heard of.
To twirling planets and exploding stars.
We reach the farthest end of the milky way and come all the way back.
We go swimming through soft clouds and hiking through tropical rainforests.

After my mama has read all the books in her bag,
We go out to search for more stories.
We find magical tales all around us.
Behind the hills.
Under our beds.
On top of the trees.

Her magic has wings.
It defies gravity and logic.
It can take you farther than any bus, train or car.

Mama says that her magic doesn't just take us to places inside stories.
It brings the characters inside the story to us.
With her magic, we can sing and dance,
Cry and laugh, run and fly with our favorite friends.
With her magic we are never alone; there are always friends floating in the magic around us.
No matter what world our friends are from or why they are here, we always have each other.

Now, my mama is teaching me how to become a Hakawati and share magic with others.
I can open a book and launch myself into the unknown, waiting for a big adventure.
I float high above the camp until my caravan looks like a speck of golden dust in a cloud of magic.

My mama taught me that when my socks get soggy,
When I am grumpy and cold,
I can use my magic to warm myself up.
I can open up a book and find myself surrounded by the warmth of my friends.
Or maybe a family of mice sneaking out to get a late night snack.
Or a snowman with an itchy back.
Or a lonely robot.
Or a cloud with a polka dots.

Would you like to experience some magic?
I can take you anywhere you like!
A beach, a mountain, a trail?
The belly of a whale?
A ship with a large sail?
You can go to all these places and more.

And after you use this magic yourself,
There is only one more thing you have to do...
Share it with everyone around you!

This was the story of two Hakawatis, Sama and Maya.
But wait! Now there are three!
Who is the third you ask?
Well, you, of course, if you are up to the task!
The magic of this story will take you far and wide.
Maybe we will meet again one day, floating in space,
or in a pirate ship race.
Until then, enjoy your magic!
And make storytelling fantastic!

CPSIA information can be obtained
at www.ICGtesting.com
Printed in the USA
BVHW011159091222
653842BV00021B/1386